AM Gratitude Galore

*The Little Pink Book of 77 Daily Declarations
to Align Your Spirit, Focus Your Mind,
and Elevate Your Life*

Copyright

AM Gratitude Galore: The Little Pink Book of 77 Daily Declarations to Align Your Spirit, Focus Your Mind, and Elevate Your Life

© 2025 Marie S. Brévil. All rights reserved. Published 2026.

No part of this publication may be reproduced, distributed, or transmitted in any form or by any means, including photocopying, recording, or other electronic or mechanical methods, without the prior written permission of the publisher, except in the case of brief quotations used in reviews or critical articles.

For permission requests, contact:
My Littl' Workshop Publishing

Cover design: MLW Studios
Interior design and layout: MLW Studios /Prince Jai/ Marie Brevil

Printed in the United States of America
First Edition, 2025

Dedication Page

I dedicate this book to me — for having the courage to continue this work, for being the realest of the realest, the best of the best. It is so easy to be discouraged, but I made the hardest choice: to continue with my work, my call, my calling. I choose to walk closely with my divinity, my power within, and to be daring in a time where society still tries to quiet outspoken women, shut them down, and proceed with plans to destroy humanity. I will not be silenced.

Together, we will continue to speak life over our own lives, the lives of our children, our families, our partners, and anyone who chooses to stand with us. We cover them and we speak life unto them.

I also dedicate this book to you — the one with the divine audacity to dare to read in a world full of distraction. Congratulations on taking a stand for yourself, relearning what matters, and using it to better your life.

So be it, and so it is.

Introduction:

Daily gratitude is more than a routine — it's a strategy for elevation. It's the armor you put on before the world can touch you. It's the way you decide that no matter what's coming, you will be rooted, radiant, and ready.

This little pink book is not just "nice words to start your day." It's a daily ignition switch for your spirit. These declarations are built to sharpen your mind, open your heart, strengthen your boundaries, and connect you to the kind of gratitude that brings real results.

Whether you read for 15 seconds or a full minute, every piece here is designed to bring you back to center and remind you who you are. This isn't about forcing positivity — it's about commanding alignment. And once you are aligned, there's nothing you cannot do.

About This Book

AM Gratitude Galore is more than a Daily read — it's a daily reset button for your spirit. This little pink book is your companion for starting each day with clarity, intention, and an unshakable focus on what truly matters.

Inside, you'll find 77 powerful Daily declarations (plus bonus ones) — each one crafted to help you center your mind, guard your energy, and step into your day with confidence and grace. Every declaration comes in three lengths — 15 seconds, 30 seconds, and 60 seconds — so whether your day is calm or chaotic, you can still pour something good into your spirit before the day begins.

This book is here to better your day, your routine, and your elevation. It's not about toxic positivity or pretending everything is fine. It's about training yourself to see solutions, not just problems. It's about building a habit of gratitude that strengthens your focus, fuels your purpose, and makes every step intentional.

Your unrelenting quest for excellence requires more than talent — it demands discipline, resilience, and discernment. Constantly pushing yourself in a positive way is worth it, but this book also reminds you not to confuse self-mastery with self-abuse. Know the difference between stretching yourself for growth and wearing yourself down for clout.

It's important to pay attention to what you're perpetuating in your daily actions. Be responsible with your energy, your time, and your intentions. Forge changes that actually move you forward. Don't let distractions, illusions, or the wrong influences derail you.

The truth is simple: life rewards solutions, not complaints. This book will help you focus on what you can build, fix, and create — and then give you the push to go get it all done.

Who Should Consider This Book & Why

This book is for you if you're ready to elevate your sunup and master your days — not just coast through them. If you want more focus, more clarity, and more control over your energy, this is your guide.

It's for those who:

- Want to be spiritual and grounded in real action.
- Refuse to sell themselves short and are ready to prioritize their divine purpose.
- Refuse to be subdued, silenced, or shut down.
- Choose to put themselves on their own pedestal instead of making everyone else the priority.
- Want to live a life they will be proud of — not one filled with regret.

This is for the doers, the dreamers, and the disciplined — the ones willing to take responsibility for their mindset and actions so they can shape their life intentionally.

How to Use This Book

These 77 AM Gratitudes are not just words to read — they're declarations to claim, believe, and live. They will only work if you agree to make them work.

Here's how to get the maximum outcome:

1. Choose one declaration each morning. Read it out loud — not in a whisper, but in a voice that carries authority and certainty.
2. Use all three lengths. Start with the 15-second version for impact, move to the 30-second to build depth, and end with the 60-second to seal it into your spirit.
3. Focus on the meaning. Don't just recite. Feel it. Picture it. Let it sink in until it becomes your truth.
4. Carry it into your day. Repeat it when you feel distracted, discouraged, or tempted to shrink back.
5. End the day with reflection. Before bed, ask yourself: Did I live this declaration today? Where did I honor it? Where can I do better tomorrow?

Sample Daily Schedule

6:30 AM – Get Up & Center
- Drink water.
- Take 2 minutes of silence to breathe deeply and set your mind for the day.

6:35 AM – Read Your Declaration
- Read the 15-second version once with energy.
- Read the 30-second version slower, with emphasis.
- Read the 60-second version as if you are speaking it into reality.

6:40 AM – Apply the Declaration
- Write one way you will live this declaration today.
- Picture yourself already doing it.

Throughout the Day – Recall & Repeat
- When stressed, distracted, or doubting, repeat the 15-second version aloud or in your mind.

Night Reflection – 5 Minutes Before Bed
- Review your day.
- Ask: Did I honor my declaration? What shifted in my energy, actions, or decisions?
- Give thanks for your wins, and set the intention to carry the same or a new declaration tomorrow.

Sample Daily Schedule ~ Now your turn

6:30 AM – _____
-
-
-

6:35 AM – _____
-
-
-

6:40 AM – _____
-
-
-

Throughout the Day – Recall & Repeat or _____
-
-
-

Night Reflection – 5 Minutes Before Bed or _____
-
-
-

~Note~

Opening Declaration

"Today, I give myself permission to rise — fully, unapologetically, and without hesitation.

I will no longer shrink to fit spaces unworthy of my light.
I will no longer delay my blessings waiting for someone else's approval.
I stand in my worth, my wisdom, and my divine timing.
I am the guardian of my peace, the keeper of my joy, and the author of my day.

I will focus on solutions, not problems.
I will see my life as sacred and worthy of my highest attention.
I am committed to speaking life into myself, prioritizing myself, and honoring myself as my first and forever responsibility.

I agree to make this work — because I know it will work for me, as long as I work it.

From this moment forward, I choose elevation, gratitude, and divine alignment above all else.

And so it is."

AM Gratitude - Some examples of what that may look like in case this is your first time working with gratitude affirmations. You can rotate them daily for AM Gratitude so it stays fresh and uplifting or you can follow the schedule here.

"Before I move, before I scroll, before I speak — I breathe and give thanks. I thank the sun for rising, the air for filling my lungs, my body for carrying me, my mind for dreaming bigger. Today is a gift, and I choose to unwrap it with gratitude."

"Every Daily is a doorway to a brand-new chapter, and I decide how I will step through it. Before the rush, before the noise, I pause to give thanks — for the breath that woke me, for the light that greets me, for the ground that holds me steady. I notice the song of the birds, the sway of the trees, the kiss of the Daily air, and I remember I am alive. Gratitude turns ordinary moments into treasures, and today I will walk in the awareness that life itself is a blessing. I honor myself, I honor my journey, and I honor the chance to do better, love deeper, and rise higher than yesterday."

"Before the world asks anything of me, I pause and give thanks. I thank the sunrise for its promise, the air for its freshness, my heart for its steady beat. I notice the small things — the light on the leaves, the quiet before the day begins — and I let them remind me that I am blessed. Gratitude shifts my energy, clears my mind, and sets my steps in alignment with goodness. Today, I rise with thanks, and I will carry that light through everything I do."

If you're in a hurry, here are some quicker ones that you can use.
Example 1
"Before I move, I thank the morning. Thank you for breath, for life, for another chance to get it right."
Example 2
"I rise with gratitude. I thank the light, the air, and my body for carrying me into a new day."
Example 3
"Gratitude is my first word today — for life, love, lessons, and the gift of right now."

Example 1

"Before the noise, I pause. I thank the sun for rising, the air for filling my lungs, and the earth for holding me steady. Every breath is a gift, and I choose to begin my day with appreciation for what is, and hope for what will be."

Example 2

"This morning, I stand still and let gratitude rise in me. I notice the softness of the air, the promise of the light, and the beating of my own heart. Today is mine to shape, and gratitude is the brush I will use."

Example 3

"I greet this day with a thankful heart. I thank my mind for dreaming, my body for waking, and my spirit for guiding me. I see blessings in the small things, and I carry that awareness forward."

~Reflection~

Example 1

"The moment I open my eyes, I remind myself — life is a gift. I breathe deeply, feeling the air fill my lungs, and thank my body for carrying me. I thank the sunrise for showing me that light always returns, and the earth for its steady presence beneath my feet. I notice the colors of the sky, the quiet hum of morning, the way life renews itself daily. Gratitude is not just a thought, it's a choice — one I make before the day unfolds. Today, I choose to walk with an open heart, see beauty in the ordinary, and honor the chance to be alive, aware, and becoming."

Example 2

"Each Daily is a new beginning, a chance to step into who I'm becoming. I thank the stillness before the world wakes, the promise in the Daily light, and the rhythm of my own breath. I remember that no matter what happened yesterday, today holds space for growth, joy, and love. Gratitude shifts my energy and makes me more present for the blessings waiting to meet me. I will walk in thankfulness, and in doing so, I will see more to be thankful for."

Example 3

"This morning, I honor the gift of being here. I thank the Creator for another sunrise, for the lessons I've learned, and the strength to keep going. I thank the wind for touching my skin, the trees for standing tall, and my heart for staying open. Gratitude teaches me to see abundance, not lack — to focus on blessings instead of burdens. I will rise with this energy, protect it, and let it guide me through every choice today."

~Reflection~

You can set up a schedule

MONDAY – New Beginnings
A.M. – "Today is a clean slate. I rise with gratitude for new chances, fresh paths, and the courage to walk them."

Mid. – "The week begins, and I choose to meet it with gratitude. I thank life for a fresh canvas, my body for the strength to create, and my mind for clarity. Today is mine to begin again."

P.M. – "Each Monday is an invitation to begin again. I thank the sun for its light, the air for its freshness, and my body for waking. I release what no longer serves me and step into this day with gratitude for the opportunities ahead. My energy is renewed, my vision is clear, and my spirit is ready for what is meant for me."

TUESDAY – Momentum

A.M. – "I give thanks for the strength to move forward. Every step today carries purpose."

Mid – "Tuesday is about movement. I thank the path beneath my feet and the will to keep going. Gratitude fuels my momentum and makes each step lighter."

P.M. – "Today, I honor progress. I give thanks for the work I've done, the lessons I've learned, and the courage to keep building. I'm grateful for the doors opening before me and for the strength to walk through them with confidence and grace."

WEDNESDAY – Alignment

A.M. – "I give thanks for balance. I walk in harmony with my purpose today."

Mid – "Midweek reminds me to check my alignment. I thank my inner voice for guiding me, and I trust that gratitude keeps me on my path."

P.M. – "On Wednesdays, I pause to align. I give thanks for my body's signals, my heart's wisdom, and the clarity that gratitude brings. I walk in balance with my goals, relationships, and spirit, trusting that I am exactly where I need to be."

THURSDAY – Abundance

A.M. – "Gratitude opens the door to abundance. I give thanks for what is and what is on its way."

Mid. – "Thursday reminds me of the blessings already here. I give thanks for my resources, my gifts, and the wealth of love and support around me."

P.M. – "Today, I celebrate abundance. I thank the Universe for the blessings that fill my life — seen and unseen. I am grateful for opportunities, for connections, and for the flow of good things into my world. My gratitude attracts more reasons to be grateful."

FRIDAY – Joy

A.M. – "Today I thank life for joy — the laughter, the music, the light in my heart."

Mid. – "Fridays remind me to dance in gratitude. I thank the week for its lessons, the people for their love, and my own spirit for staying vibrant."

P.M – "I greet this Friday with joy. I thank life for the laughter I've shared, the kindness I've received, and the strength I've shown. My heart is light because I choose to see beauty in the small things. I let gratitude be my song today."

SATURDAY – Restoration

A.M. – "I thank this day for rest, renewal, and peace in my soul."

Mid. – "Saturday is my day to restore. I give thanks for stillness, for the body that carries me, and for the chance to refuel my spirit."

P.M. – "Today, I slow down. I thank my body for its resilience, my mind for its clarity, and my heart for its strength. Saturday is my reminder that rest is productive and necessary. I let gratitude wash over me like a soft stream, restoring my energy."

SUNDAY – Spiritual Renewal

15s – "I thank the Creator for life, love, and another chance to shine my light."

30s – "Sunday is a sacred pause. I thank my breath, my blessings, and the Source that sustains me. Gratitude reconnects me to my highest self."

60s – "This Sunday, I honor the gift of being alive. I thank the Creator for another sunrise, for the strength to overcome, and for the love that flows through me. I am grateful for guidance, for clarity, and for the vision of the path ahead. Today, I rest in trust, knowing I am held and guided."

~Reflection~

Gratitude Galore

"Gratitude galore — I bless our situation, this generation, our wisdom, our elevation, our frequency. Pure vibes only. I bless, guard, and shield our vibrations. Grace and mercy lead the way, and love is always my comfort. I am grateful for the way this day progresses, for I know already that all is well and all is working out for my highest good."

AM Reflection Prompt

"Before the world reaches for me, I reach within. The first thing I do when I rise is take time to reflect — to notice where I am, who I'm becoming, and what I'm grateful for. Reflection roots me, gratitude lifts me, and from there, I am ready for the day."

~Reflection~

A Flexible Daily Rhythm (Use What Fits Your Life)

This book is designed to support you where you are, not to pressure you into perfection. Your day may look different depending on your work, responsibilities, or season of life — and that is okay.

AM — 15 Seconds (Set the Tone)

Mornings are often rushed. This is why the 15-second declaration exists — to give you a moment of grounding before the world demands your attention. Use this when you first wake up, before reaching for your phone, or even while getting ready. It's not about how long — it's about intention.

Midday — 30 Seconds (Reset & Recenter)

By midday, there is usually a little more patience — or a greater need for a pick-me-up.

Use the 30-second declaration to:

- Reset your focus
- Calm your nervous system
- Remind yourself why you're doing what you're doing

This can be done during a break, while walking, in your car, or between tasks.

PM — 60 Seconds (Seal the Day)

Evenings tend to offer more time for reflection.
The 60-second declaration allows you to:

- Slow down
- Release the day
- Restore your energy through gratitude

This is ideal before bed, during your wind-down routine, or in quiet solitude.

Important Reminder

This is not a one-size-fits-all rule.

If you work overnight, your "AM" may begin at night.
If your schedule shifts, adjust the rhythm to match your life.
What matters is not the clock — but the consistency.

Choose what works:

- One declaration a day
- Two if you have the space
- All three when life allows

There is no failure here — only return.

This practice works if you agree to work it.

Not perfectly.
Not rigidly.
But honestly and intentionally.

Your life is sacred.
Use these words to support it — not to pressure it.

1.

Take Time to Reflect. Gratitude.

A.M. - "The first thing I do each Daily is pause and reflect. Gratitude fills me before the day begins, centering my mind and heart."

Mid. - "When I rise, I take time to reflect before anything else. I breathe in stillness, notice where I am, and give thanks for life, lessons, and possibilities. This moment of gratitude sets the tone for a peaceful, purposeful day."

P.M. "Before the world asks anything of me, I take time to reflect. I sit in stillness, breathing deeply, allowing gratitude to rise in me. I notice how far I've come, the lessons I've learned, and the blessings already present. Reflection grounds me, gratitude lifts me, and together they prepare me for the day ahead. By choosing to begin with this sacred pause, I align my mind, body, and spirit with clarity, purpose, and joy."

~Reflection~

2.

Gratitude Galore. Gratitude.

A.M. - "Gratitude galore — I bless our situation, our generation, our wisdom, our elevation. Grace and mercy lead the way, and love is always my comfort."

Mid. - "Gratitude galore — I bless our situation, this generation, our wisdom, our elevation, and our frequency. I guard and shield our vibrations, keeping them pure. Grace and mercy lead the way, and love is always my comfort. I am grateful for how the day unfolds for my highest good."

P.M. - "Gratitude galore — I bless our situation, this generation, our wisdom, our elevation, and our frequency. Pure vibes flow through me as I guard, shield, and protect our vibrations. Grace and mercy lead the way, and love is always my comfort. I give thanks for the way this day progresses, knowing already that all is well, all is aligned, and all is working out for my highest good. My gratitude fills the space ahead of me, ensuring that everything I touch, everything I speak, and everything I attract is in harmony with the life I am creating."

~Reflection~

3.

Be Grateful for the Small Things. Gratitude.

A.M. - "Many are 'successful' yet not happy. I choose gratitude for the little things, remembering I once prayed for what I have today."

Mid. - "So many people seem successful, yet still feel empty. I choose to see and give thanks for the little things — the smile, the breath, the moment of peace — because I remember when these were prayers. Gratitude for the small makes room for the greater blessings still to come."

P.M. - "There are so many people who appear successful yet live without joy. I will not let my life be like that. I take time to notice and be grateful for the little things — the warmth of sunlight, the kindness of a friend, the strength in my own body — because I remember when these moments, comforts, and opportunities were prayers on my lips. My gratitude for the small things creates space for the bigger blessings that are on their way. I honor what I have now, knowing it is the foundation for all I will receive."

~Reflection~

4.

Focus on Your Own Shine. Gratitude.

A.M. - "Not all that shines today will shine tomorrow. I focus on my truth, my light, my growth — never selling myself short for the temporary."

Mid. - "In life, not all that shines today will keep shining. I stay grounded in my truth, grateful for what sustains me. I refuse to sell myself short for temporary promises. My focus, gratitude, and patience allow me to accomplish anything. I tend my own shine, my own grass, my own energy."

P.M. - "I remind myself daily: not all that shines today will shine forever. I know my truth, I know what keeps me afloat, and I never sell myself short for temporary situations or empty promises. I am capable of anything when I focus, stay grateful, and move with patience. My journey is mine, my growth is sacred, and my shine is my own. I do not waste my energy comparing my grass to another's. I water what is mine, and in doing so, I flourish beyond measure."

~Reflection~

From Overlooked to Gratitude. Gratitude.

A.M. - "What I once overlooked was always there. Today, I pay attention — and I am deeply grateful for what I now see."

Mid. - "Sometimes I miss what's right in front of me. Then life places me in a moment where I have no choice but to pay attention. What I once thought wasn't there has been here all along. Today, I see it, I feel it, and I'm in the deepest gratitude for it."

P.M. - "Some days, you look at something and it feels like nothing is there — only because you weren't truly paying attention. Then life shifts, and you're placed in a situation where attention is no longer optional. You notice, you see, you realize that what you thought was missing had been there all along, waiting for you to acknowledge it. And here you are, standing in that moment, wrapped in the deepest gratitude for what was always yours. Today, I honor what I see, what I know, and what I had all along."

~Reflection~

6.

Keep Going – Gratitude & Resilience.

A.M. - "Some people will leave when your light shines. I keep going, knowing my kindness and integrity are enough for me, even if not for them."

Mid. - "Some days, I wonder what happened to the friends I thought I had. But I keep going. I know some people create stories about me, get uncomfortable when I grow, or walk with demons that can't stand my light. My kindness, generosity, and spiritual integrity are enough, even if they choose to leave."

P.M. - "Some days, I rise and wonder what happened to the people I thought were my friends. Now here I am, under the sun, realizing that no matter what, I must keep going. People often create characters for you, get upset when you break out of their box, or carry demons that will never allow them to stay too close to your light. Even if the whole world can see that I've done nothing but be kind, some will still act funny, ghost me, or disappear. The truth is — for those who lack spiritual integrity, kindness and generosity will never be enough. But I will keep shining, keep moving forward, and remain grateful for the ones who can walk in the light with me."

~Reflection~

7.

Authorize Your Freedom – Gratitude.

A.M. - "I don't wait for permission to live. I walk alone when I must, invest in myself, and make my presence valuable."

Mid - "Sometimes the best thing you can do is take a walk alone in the early morning. Don't wait for permission — you are the one who can authorize your freedom. When you are always available in friendship or love, people may forget to value you. So I make myself rare, and I invest my time in myself."

P.M. - "There are mornings when the wisest choice is to walk alone. I don't wait for someone to grant me permission to live my life — I am the one who authorizes my freedom. I've learned that when I am too available in friendship or even in love, people can forget my worth or take my presence for granted. So I make myself rare, I set boundaries, and I use that time to invest in my own growth, healing, and joy. My gratitude is for the solitude that strengthens me and the self-respect that keeps me free."

~Reflection~

8.

Own Your Daily – Gratitude.

A.M. - "The Daily is mine to claim. I rise with intention, gratitude, and the power to set the tone for my entire day."

Mid. - "The Daily belongs to me, and I choose to own it. I rise with gratitude, letting the first thoughts I think be ones that align me with joy and clarity. Each sunrise is an invitation to create a day I will be proud of."

P.M. - "Every morning, I remind myself — this time is mine to claim. I own it before the world takes a piece of me. I rise with gratitude for the breath in my lungs, the light on my skin, and the opportunity to shape my day with intention. My thoughts set my direction, and my gratitude fuels my strength. I do not rush into chaos; I step into peace, clarity, and focus, knowing this choice shapes everything that follows."

~Reflection~

9.

Walk with the Day – Gratitude.

A.M. - "The day is a path and I am the traveler. I walk with gratitude, letting the wind teach me, the sun guide me, and the earth hold me steady."

Mid. - "The day unfolds like a path beneath my feet, and I am both the traveler and the witness. I walk in gratitude, feeling the wind whisper truths, the sun warm my spirit, and the earth carry my steps. Life is not to be rushed — it is to be walked with presence and thanks."

P.M. - "The day greets me like a trail through the forest — winding, alive, full of whispers I can only hear if I move with awareness. I am the traveler, the listener, and the witness. The wind teaches me release, the sun reminds me of my own warmth, and the earth tells me I am always supported. Gratitude is the pace I keep; presence is the compass I follow. I walk with the day, not ahead of it, not behind it, but with it — honoring each step as a gift, each moment as part of my becoming."

~Reflection~

10.

Sunrise Within – Gratitude.

A.M. - "The sun rises outside, but it also rises in me. I greet this light with gratitude, letting it awaken every corner of my soul."

Mid. - "The sunrise does not rush — it arrives with quiet certainty. I, too, rise in my own time, carrying light into the day. I give thanks for this slow unveiling, for the warmth that touches my skin and the hope that stirs within. I am the sunrise; I am the light."

P.M. - "The world is still as the first gold spills across the horizon. The sun does not ask permission to rise; it simply fulfills its purpose. I feel its warmth touch my skin, its light awaken my spirit. In this moment, I remember — I am also a sunrise. I am meant to rise, to shine, to bring light to what I touch. My gratitude deepens with every breath, for the chance to begin again, for the beauty of presence, for the truth that no matter how dark the night, the light will always return. And today, that light begins with me."

~Reflection~

11.

Rain as Renewal – Gratitude.

A.M. - "The rain does not apologize for falling. I thank it for cleansing the earth, and I let it remind me to cleanse my own spirit."

Mid. - "Daily rain drapes the world in silver. I give thanks for the water that feeds the earth, for the way it washes away dust and makes room for growth. I, too, allow myself to be renewed — to release what no longer serves and welcome what is fresh and true."

P.M. - "The rain comes softly, yet with purpose, touching every leaf, every stone, every rooftop. It does not seek permission; it simply falls, cleansing what is and nourishing what will be. I stand in gratitude for this reminder that renewal often comes quietly. Just as the rain frees the earth from dust, I free my heart from what weighs it down. I release yesterday's heaviness and make space for new seeds to take root. Today, I am washed, I am renewed, I am ready."

~Reflection~

12.

Stand Like a Mountain – Gratitude.

A.M. - "Like the mountain, I stand tall. Winds may howl, storms may pass, but my roots hold steady in gratitude."

Mid. - "The mountain does not bow to the storm. It stands, holding centuries of sunrises, storms, and stillness in its frame. I give thanks for the strength within me that, like the mountain, remains unshaken — grounded in gratitude, no matter what comes."

P.M. - "The mountain greets each day with the same quiet power — whether bathed in golden light or cloaked in heavy clouds. It knows the storms will pass, the winds will still, and the sun will return. I, too, carry that knowing. My gratitude is my root system, reaching deep into the soil of my being, keeping me steady in joy and in challenge. No matter the weather in my life, I stand in my truth, I rise in my power, and I endure in grace. Like the mountain, I am timeless, I am steady, I am here."

~Reflection~

13.

Flow Like the Ocean – Gratitude.

A.M. - "Like the ocean, I rise and fall, yet I am never lost. My gratitude keeps me flowing toward all that is meant for me."

Mid. - "The ocean moves without fear of its tides. I give thanks for the waves that carry me forward, for the depths that remind me of my strength, and for the constant renewal that life offers when I trust the flow."

P.M. - "The ocean speaks in rhythms — tides that rise, tides that fall, each one a reminder that nothing in life is stagnant. I stand in gratitude for my own ability to move with the currents, to release when it's time, and to receive when blessings flow in. Like the sea, I am vast, I am deep, and I am connected to everything. Every wave is a lesson in letting go and returning. Every horizon is a promise of more to come. Today, I flow in gratitude, knowing that the tides of life always carry me where I am meant to be."

~Reflection~

14.

Grow Like the Forest – Gratitude.

A.M. - "The forest grows in silence, yet thrives. I am grateful for the strength I gain in the quiet places of my life."

Mid. - "The forest does not rush to prove itself. It grows, rooted and steady, letting time and nature do their work. I give thanks for the quiet growth within me — for the patience, the strength, and the unseen miracles that shape my path."

P.M. - "The forest teaches me that growth is not always loud or visible. Trees rise slowly, roots stretch deep, and stillness feeds life just as surely as rain and sun. I am grateful for the hidden work happening in me — the lessons being absorbed, the strength being built, the wisdom taking root. I trust my process, even when it's unseen. Like the forest, I grow in my own season, standing tall in gratitude for every step along the way."

~Reflection~

15.

Preserve Your Light – Gratitude.

A.M. - "It is my responsibility to guard my life, my heart, and my time. Gratitude fuels my strength, protection keeps my peace."

Mid. - "It's my duty to shield my life, my heart, and my time. People may show up when they need me, but not all have pure intentions. Gratitude keeps me grounded, protection keeps me safe, and I choose to preserve my peace."

P.M. - "It is my responsibility to ensure that my life, my heart, and my time are protected. Some will give me their presence when it benefits them, yet quietly hold the heart of a traitor. I don't dwell in suspicion, for I am spiritual and I know better, but I also stay aware. I work hard to create a reality filled with joy and truth, yet from time to time, one or two will slip in trying to disturb that experience. It is up to me to guard my energy, to preserve my peace, and to protect the quality of my days. Gratitude is my shield, awareness is my armor, and my light will not be dimmed."

~Reflection~

16.

Discernment & Openness – Gratitude.

A.M. - "Discernment is divine. I stay open to blessings, but I protect my spirit. I welcome what's for me, and release what is not."

Mid. - "Discernment is a sacred key — it helps me protect my peace and still remain open to life's blessings. Many miss out on what was meant for them because they were too guarded. I choose balance: I stay aware, but I stay open. I receive with gratitude and wisdom."

P.M. - "Discernment is not about shutting people out — it's about honoring the truth of what aligns. In this life, you must be able to recognize what feeds your growth and what silently drains it. Many blessings are missed not because they weren't sent, but because the heart wasn't open to receive. I rise today with clear eyes and an open heart. I protect my spirit, but I do not harden it. I welcome the good that is meant for me, and I release what isn't with peace. Gratitude leads the way, and discernment keeps me steady."

~Reflection~

17.

Trusting Myself Again – Gratitude.

A.M. - "Even when others failed me, I choose to trust myself again. I rise with gratitude for my resilience and inner wisdom."

Mid. - "There were times I trusted the wrong people and blamed myself for it. But this morning, I give thanks for the lessons and the strength I gained. I choose to trust myself again — my intuition, my voice, my knowing. I walk forward with gratitude and grace."

P.M. - "Some mornings I remember the people who disappointed me — those I trusted too soon, too deeply. And for a while, I questioned myself more than them. But today, I give thanks for the wisdom I gained. I reclaim my power, my voice, and my ability to choose better going forward. I forgive myself for not knowing then what I know now. I trust myself again — not because I'm perfect, but because I've grown. And that, in itself, is something to be grateful for."

~Reflection~

18.

Reclaiming Joy – Gratitude.

A.M. - "Joy is mine. I don't wait for permission to feel it. I choose it now, in this breath, in this rising."

Mid. - "This morning, I reclaim my joy. Not because everything is perfect — but because I am allowed to feel good anyway. I give thanks for laughter, for music, for the warmth in my chest. My joy is sacred, and I rise in it fully."

P.M. - "Today, I give myself permission to reclaim joy — not the kind that needs to be earned, but the kind that simply exists. I don't wait for a special moment or flawless circumstances. Joy is here in the sunlight, in the stillness, in the fact that I made it through and I'm still rising. I give thanks for the smile that comes back to my face, for the giggle that returns to my chest, and for the truth that joy is not selfish — it's survival. And I intend to survive beautifully."

~Reflection~

Making Peace with the Past – Gratitude.

A.M. - "I release what no longer belongs to my present. I rise with peace in my heart and gratitude in my spirit."

Mid. - "The past can't hold me hostage. I acknowledge it, I thank it for the lessons, and I let it be what it was. I make peace with it so I can walk fully into my today — whole, grounded, and grateful."

P.M. - "There are things I wish I could change. Words I said. Moments I missed. But I am not here to relive the past — I am here to rise. I choose to make peace with what has been. I hold space for what it taught me and I release the rest. My gratitude today is not just for what I have, but for what I've survived. The past shaped me, but it does not define me. I give thanks for today — a new chance to live lighter, love deeper, and rise freer."

~Reflection~

20.

Choosing Myself First – Gratitude.

A.M. - "Today, I choose me — not out of guilt, but out of truth. I am my own priority, and that is sacred."

Mid. - "I no longer feel guilty for choosing myself. My peace, my purpose, my joy matter. I rise today with gratitude for the freedom to put myself first — not to exclude others, but to finally include myself fully."

P.M. - "There was a time I called it selfish to put myself first — now I call it sacred. I've poured into others, delayed my own needs, and dimmed my light to make others comfortable. No more. Today, I rise in gratitude for the wisdom to honor my own soul first. Choosing myself isn't rejection — it's remembrance. I remember my worth, my purpose, and my responsibility to love me first. And with that, everything else can rise in alignment."

~Reflection~

21.

Divine Timing – Gratitude.

A.M. - "Divine timing is everything. I release the rush and give thanks for what is arriving right on time."

Mid. - "Many mistakes are made when I try to force what only divine timing can deliver. Today, I rise in peace and give thanks for the perfect unfolding of all things. I trust the delays, the pauses, the alignment — because divine timing never fails."

P.M. - "Divine timing is everything — not my ego's rush, not the pressure of the world, but the sacred rhythm that governs all things. So many times, I've stumbled by trying to make things happen my way, my time. But now I know better. I release the need to control and instead walk in gratitude for the divine order working behind the scenes. What is mine will find me. What is meant will not miss me. And I will not let delay make me doubt. Today, I rise with trust, I move with patience, and I align with the divine."

~Reflection~

22.

Trust the Unseen Path – Gratitude.

A.M. - "Even when I can't see the whole path, I trust the steps. Gratitude keeps me moving, faith keeps me steady."

Mid. - "In this life and the next, whatever that may be, I trust the unseen path. I don't need to see every turn to know I am guided. I give thanks for the light in each step, even when the destination is still hidden."

P.M. - "In this life and the next, whatever that may be, I trust the unseen path. I know the way may not always reveal itself all at once — and that's alright. I give thanks for the guidance I can't always name, for the gentle nudge forward when I feel unsure. My faith is not dependent on seeing the end; it is anchored in knowing I am not walking alone. Today, I step forward in gratitude for the mystery, the lessons, and the beauty that reveal themselves only when the time is right."

~Reflection~

23.

Resilience, Beauty, and Being – Gratitude.

A.M. - "I give thanks for my resilience, for the beauty that shifts my heart, and for the courage to be who I truly am."

Mid. - "Without resilience, life would not be the same. I give thanks for the strength to keep going, for the beauty that changes how I see the world, and for the courage to be who I am meant to be — even when others want me to be something else."

P.M. - "I rise today in gratitude for my resilience — the quiet, unshakable strength that has carried me through moments I thought I would not survive. I give thanks for beauty, for in beauty my heart softens, my vision clears, and my emotions shift toward what is good. And I am deeply grateful for the courage to be who and what I truly am, because it is not always easy to walk in authenticity when the world tries to shape you into its version of you. Today, I honor my strength, I honor my sight, and I honor my truth."

~Reflection~

24.

Gratitude for What Infuses Me – Gratitude.

A.M. - "I give thanks for what infuses me with life. My boundaries are sacred altars — to be honored, not crossed."

Mid. - "I am grateful for what fills me, not what drains me. No more enabling, no more pretending. My boundaries are altars — inevitable, irrevocable, and to be respected without exception. They are not walls to block love, but gates to protect my peace."

P.M. - "I rise in gratitude for what infuses me — for the people, spaces, and choices that pour into my spirit instead of pulling from it. No more enabling. No more games. My boundaries are not flimsy walls or suggestions; they are sacred altars. They must be honored, respected, and upheld — inevitably, irrespectively, irrevocably. They are not meant to block out love or connection, but to guard the sanctity of my peace, my joy, and my life. Today, I walk with the deep knowing that what is meant for me will honor my altars, not try to tear them down."

~Reflection~

25.

Gratitude for Alignment – Gratitude.

A.M. - "I give thanks for alignment — for what matches my energy and honors my truth without force or compromise."

Mid. - "I am grateful for alignment, for the way it draws the right people, places, and opportunities into my life. I no longer chase or beg; what is meant for me arrives ready to honor my truth and my boundaries."

P.M. - "Today, I give thanks for alignment — that divine order where what is meant for me already speaks my language and matches my frequency. I do not have to shrink, bend, or bargain for what is aligned. It arrives with respect for my boundaries, recognition of my worth, and harmony with my spirit. Alignment frees me from the exhaustion of chasing and allows me to rest in the knowing that what is truly mine will meet me as I am, honor me as I am, and grow with me as I rise."

~Reflection~

26.

Gratitude for the Sun – Gratitude.

A.M. - "I give thanks for the sun that rises every day, reminding me I matter, I have power, and I can do better through grace."

Mid. - "The sun rises without fail, even when the world is not perfect. It reminds me that I matter, that I have quiet power, and that I can choose to do better. I give thanks for this daily grace, and for the chance to live with intention and gratitude."

P.M. - "Each morning, the sun rises — whether skies are clear or storms remain. It never questions its worth, and in its light, I remember mine. The sun shows me that I matter, that I am still in power, that I can choose to do better if I am willing. It carries that quiet confidence, the kind that asks for no applause, only presence. And through its constancy, it teaches me to have intentions in all that I do. Today, I rise in gratitude for who I am, for what I have survived, and for the grace that carries me — just as the sun carries the day."

~Reflection~

27.

Gratitude for the Moon – Gratitude.

A.M. - "I thank the moon for its quiet light, reminding me that even in darkness, I can still shine."

Mid. - "The moon rises without noise, bathing the night in silver calm. It teaches me that light doesn't need to be loud to be powerful. I give thanks for this reminder and for the peace it brings."

P.M. - "The moon appears each night, steady in its cycles, teaching me the beauty of change and the strength of quiet light. It shows me that even in darkness, there is a glow to guide the way. I give thanks for its gentle presence, for the peace it inspires, and for the reminder that power can be soft, grace can be steady, and every phase has its purpose."

~Reflection~

28.

Gratitude for Release – Gratitude.

A.M. - "I am grateful for the beauty of letting go. I release without bitterness, making space for what is meant to be."

Mid. - "Letting go is not losing — it is opening my hands for what is next. I give thanks for the peace that comes when I release without bitterness, trusting the space will be filled with better."

P.M. - "Release is a sacred act. I let go not in anger, but in trust. I am grateful for the strength to free myself from what no longer serves, and for the wisdom to know that space must be cleared for new blessings to enter. I release without bitterness, keeping my heart open for what is meant for me, and my spirit light enough to rise when called."

~Reflection~

29.

Daily Courage to Face the Unknown – Gratitude.

A.M. - "I greet the unknown with courage. Gratitude turns uncertainty into possibility."

Mid. - "The unknown does not scare me — it calls me to rise. I give thanks for the courage to step into what I cannot yet see, trusting that grace walks with me."

P.M. - "Each new day holds mysteries I cannot predict, paths I cannot yet see. But instead of fearing the unknown, I greet it with courage. I am grateful for the strength to take the next step, even when the way ahead is uncertain. I trust that every step is guided, every twist has purpose, and every unknown holds the potential for beauty. Gratitude is my anchor, courage is my compass, and together they carry me forward."

~Reflection~

30.

Gratitude for Self-Forgiveness – Gratitude.

A.M. - "I give thanks for the grace to forgive myself, releasing guilt and walking lighter into today."

Mid. - "This morning, I forgive myself — for what I knew and didn't know, for what I did and didn't do. I give thanks for the grace that allows me to release guilt and walk lighter into the day."

P.M. - "I rise with gratitude for self-forgiveness. I forgive myself for the mistakes I made when I didn't know better, and for the times I knew better but still fell short. I release the heavy chains of guilt, choosing instead to walk lighter into today. Forgiving myself does not erase the past, but it redeems my present. It makes space for healing, growth, and the grace to try again."

~Reflection~

31.

Gratitude for Divine Protection – Gratitude.

A.M. - "I am grateful for divine protection — seen and unseen — that shields me in every step I take."

Mid. - "Every morning, I give thanks for divine protection that surrounds me — from dangers I see and from those I never even know about. I walk today covered, guided, and safe."

P.M. - "I give thanks for divine protection — for the unseen shields around me, the closed doors that spared me harm, and the gentle redirections that led me to safer ground. I am grateful for the hand of grace that guards my path, for the whispers that steer me away from trouble, and for the light that follows me wherever I go. Today, I walk knowing I am covered, guided, and safe."

~Reflection~

32.

Gratitude for Answered Prayers – Gratitude.

A.M. - "I give thanks for every answered prayer — even the ones that came differently than I expected."

Mid. - "This morning, I am grateful for answered prayers. Some came just as I asked, others in ways I could not have imagined. All arrived in divine timing, and for that, I give thanks."

P.M. - "I rise today in gratitude for every answered prayer — the ones that came swiftly and the ones that took their time. I thank the Creator for the blessings that matched my requests and for those that came disguised as challenges but revealed themselves as greater gifts. I give thanks for the patience to wait and for the wisdom to see that every answer, whether yes, no, or not yet, is part of my perfect path."

~Reflection~

33.

Gratitude for Strength in Waiting Seasons – Gratitude.

A.M. - "I thank the Creator for giving me strength while I wait, knowing that waiting is not wasted."

Mid. - "Waiting is not punishment — it's preparation. I give thanks for the strength, patience, and hope I receive while I wait for what is meant for me."

P.M. - "There are seasons where the answer is not yet, where the vision is clear but the timing has not arrived. In these moments, I give thanks for the strength to keep standing, for the patience to keep believing, and for the faith to keep preparing. Waiting is not wasted time — it is sacred ground where roots deepen and character grows. I trust that when the moment comes, I will be ready because I was willing to wait."

~Reflection~

34.

Gratitude for New Opportunities – Gratitude.

A.M. - "I give thanks for new opportunities, knowing each one holds the power to change my life for the better."

Mid. - "Today, I am grateful for every new opportunity — the ones I've worked for and the ones that arrive unexpectedly. I welcome them with readiness, faith, and an open heart."

P.M. - "This morning, I give thanks for new opportunities — the doors that open, the calls that come, the unexpected invitations that change the course of my life. Some opportunities are the fruits of long labor, and others arrive as gifts of grace. I am grateful for the wisdom to recognize them, the courage to embrace them, and the readiness to step into them fully."

~Reflection~

35.

Gratitude for Lessons Learned from Challenges – Gratitude.

A.M. - "I thank every challenge for the lessons it taught me, for they shaped the strength I carry today."

Mid. - "Challenges are not here to destroy me, but to reveal my strength. I give thanks for the wisdom gained from every trial I've endured."

P.M. - "Every challenge I've faced has left me with a lesson — sometimes hard-earned, sometimes quietly understood. I give thanks for the storms that built my endurance, for the setbacks that redirected my steps, and for the obstacles that sharpened my vision. I am stronger, wiser, and more grounded because of what I have overcome. Today, I rise in gratitude for every trial that became my teacher."

~Reflection~

36.

Gratitude for Clarity – Gratitude.

A.M. - "I give thanks for clarity — the light that helps me see the truth and choose my next step with confidence."

Mid. - "Clarity is a gift I do not take for granted. I give thanks for the light it brings, for the noise it silences, and for the way it guides me toward what is right for me."

P.M. - "This morning, I give thanks for clarity — for the moments when the fog lifts, when the answer becomes clear, when my next step feels sure. Clarity is not just seeing — it is knowing. It strips away confusion, silences doubt, and illuminates the path that aligns with my truth. I am grateful for the wisdom to recognize it and the courage to follow where it leads."

~Reflection~

37.

Gratitude for Unexpected Blessings – Gratitude.

A.M. - "I am grateful for unexpected blessings — proof that the universe works in my favor in ways I can't imagine."

Mid. - "Some blessings come planned, others arrive like surprises wrapped in grace. I give thanks for the unexpected ones, knowing they are often the sweetest."

P.M. - "I rise today in gratitude for unexpected blessings — the ones I didn't see coming, the ones that slipped quietly into my life and changed it for the better. They remind me that the universe is always working behind the scenes on my behalf, aligning people, moments, and opportunities I could not have orchestrated on my own. I welcome these surprises with an open heart, knowing they are signs of love, favor, and divine alignment."

~Reflection~

38.

Gratitude for Health – Gratitude.

A.M. - "I give thanks for my health, for the strength in my body, and for the breath that sustains me today."

Mid. - "Health is a gift I will never take for granted. I give thanks for the strength in my body, the energy in my spirit, and the breath that allows me to live this day fully."

P.M. - "This morning, I give thanks for my health — for the miracle of my heartbeat, the steady rhythm of my breath, and the strength in my body. Health allows me to show up for my life, to care for those I love, and to pursue the purpose I was created for. Even on days when I am healing or growing stronger, I remain grateful for the vessel that carries my spirit."

~Reflection~

Gratitude for Loving Connections – Gratitude.

A.M. - "I give thanks for the love that surrounds me, in every form it takes, near and far."

Mid. - "I am grateful for the loving connections in my life — for those who see me, honor me, and walk with me through every season."

P.M. - "This morning, I give thanks for love — the kind that is steady, true, and nourishing. I am grateful for the connections that lift me up, for the people who see my worth, for the moments of laughter, understanding, and care. Love is not always loud, but it is always felt. Today, I choose to cherish it, nurture it, and let it flow freely from me to others."

~Reflection~

40.

Gratitude for Creative Inspiration – Gratitude.

A.M. - "I give thanks for creative sparks that light my mind and open new paths for expression."

Mid. - "I am grateful for the gift of creativity — for the ideas, visions, and solutions that flow into my mind and bring beauty into the world."

P.M. - "This morning, I give thanks for creative inspiration — those sparks that appear in moments of stillness or bursts of energy, guiding me to create, build, and express. Creativity is more than art; it is the ability to solve problems, to imagine better ways, to bring something into existence that wasn't there before. I honor these ideas as divine gifts, and I move through my day ready to make them real."

~Reflection~

Gratitude for Rest – Gratitude.

A.M. - "I give thanks for the rest that renews me, knowing it is essential for my strength and clarity."

Mid. - "Rest is not weakness — it is restoration. I give thanks for the sleep, pauses, and still moments that allow me to rise ready and strong."

P.M. - "I rise today in gratitude for rest — the deep, renewing stillness that restores my body, mind, and spirit. Rest is not a luxury; it is a sacred requirement for my well-being. I honor my need for sleep, for quiet, for moments of pause throughout the day. In rest, I find clarity. In rest, I rebuild my strength. In rest, I prepare myself to live fully."

~Reflection~

42.

Gratitude for Nature – Gratitude.

A.M. - "I give thanks for nature's beauty, for it reminds me that life is abundant, alive, and ever-renewing."

Mid. - "I am grateful for the trees, the sky, the wind, the water — for the way nature grounds me and shows me that there is a rhythm to life beyond my own."

P.M. - "This morning, I give thanks for nature — for the gentle sway of the trees, the soft touch of the wind, the steady flow of water, and the vast expanse of the sky. Nature reminds me that life is always renewing, always moving forward. It grounds me in the present moment while whispering of infinite possibilities. In nature, I find peace, clarity, and the courage to keep growing."

~Reflection~

43.

Gratitude for Personal Growth – Gratitude.

A.M. - "I give thanks for how far I've come, and for the growth that continues to shape me."

Mid. - "I am grateful for every step of my growth — the easy ones and the hard ones — for they have built the person I am today."

P.M. - "This morning, I give thanks for my personal growth — for the small steps, the great leaps, and even the moments that felt like stillness but were quietly transforming me. I honor the lessons learned, the old patterns released, and the new truths embraced. Growth is not always comfortable, but it is always worth it. I am grateful for the way it has shaped me into someone stronger, wiser, and more aligned with my purpose."

~Reflection~

44.

Gratitude for Wisdom & Alchemy – Gratitude.

A.M. - "I give thanks for being wiser, stronger, and an alchemist of my own life — turning every lesson into gold."

Mid. - "I am grateful for the wisdom I carry, the strength I embody, and the alchemy I've mastered. I am not just someone who's been hurt or angry — I am the one who transforms life's lessons into light."

P.M. - "This morning, I give thanks for the wisdom that has grown from my experiences — for the way I have become smarter, stronger, and a true alchemist of my life. I am no longer defined by anger or pain, but by the ability to transform challenges into wisdom, wounds into strength, and lessons into blessings. My words carry power, my mind carries brilliance, and my heart carries infinite gratitude for the person I have become. Every step, every trial, every moment has shaped me into someone who not only survives but thrives."

~Reflection~

45.

Gratitude for Wisdom – Gratitude.

A.M. - "I give thanks for the wisdom that guides me, born from lessons learned and truth embraced."

Mid. - "I am grateful for the wisdom I carry — the insight shaped by experience, the clarity sharpened by truth, and the discernment that protects my path."

P.M. - "This morning, I give thanks for wisdom — for the deep knowing that comes from living, learning, and listening to the truth within. Wisdom is not just what I know, but how I apply it. It is the quiet voice that says, 'This way.' It is the shield that keeps me from repeating old mistakes, and the lantern that lights my way forward. I honor every lesson that brought me here, and I walk in gratitude for the wisdom that continues to grow."

~Reflection~

46.

Gratitude for Peace of Mind – Gratitude.

A.M. - "I am grateful for peace of mind, for it is the foundation on which joy and clarity are built."

Mid. - "Peace of mind is a treasure beyond measure. I give thanks for the calm in my spirit, the clarity in my thoughts, and the stillness that allows me to hear my own heart."

P.M. - "This morning, I give thanks for peace of mind — the priceless calm that allows me to live with intention and joy. It is the soft space where my thoughts settle, where my spirit feels safe, and where my decisions are made from clarity instead of chaos. I guard this peace, I nurture it, and I honor it as the foundation for everything I build. With peace of mind, I can see clearly, love deeply, and live fully."

~Reflection~

47.

Gratitude for Abundance – Gratitude.

A.M. - "I give thanks for the abundance flowing into my life — in love, in resources, and in opportunity."

Mid. - "Abundance is all around me. I give thanks for the love, resources, opportunities, and blessings that continue to multiply in my life."

P.M. - "This morning, I give thanks for abundance — for the overflowing love in my life, the resources that meet my needs, and the opportunities that expand my world. Abundance is not only material; it is the joy I feel, the peace I hold, and the relationships I cherish. I welcome more with an open heart, knowing that gratitude is the magnet that draws it closer."

~Reflection~

48.

Gratitude for Divine Guidance – Gratitude.

A.M. - "I give thanks for divine guidance that leads me exactly where I need to be."

Mid. - "I am grateful for the divine guidance that speaks to me in whispers, signs, and moments of clarity, always leading me toward my highest good."

P.M. - "This morning, I give thanks for divine guidance — for the unseen hand that directs my steps, the quiet whispers that steer me, and the signs that reassure me I am on the right path. Even when I don't see the full picture, I trust that I am being led toward my highest good. I honor this guidance by listening, by trusting, and by moving with faith."

~Reflection~

49.

Gratitude for Faith – Gratitude.

A.M. - "I give thanks for my faith — the anchor that keeps me steady when the waves of life rise."

Mid. - "Faith keeps me moving even when I can't see the full path ahead. I give thanks for the trust that holds me steady in every season of life."

P.M. - "This morning, I give thanks for my faith — the quiet strength that steadies me in uncertainty, the light that guides me when I cannot see far ahead. Faith is my anchor and my compass. It tells me that even when the way is unclear, I am still moving in the right direction. I honor this gift by holding on, believing, and walking forward in trust."

~Reflection~

50.

Gratitude for Persistence – Gratitude.

A.M. - "I give thanks for my persistence — the will to keep going when the road gets hard."

Mid. - "Persistence has carried me through storms and challenges. I give thanks for the strength to keep showing up, even when progress feels slow."

P.M. - "This morning, I give thanks for persistence — the steady, determined spirit that refuses to give up. I am grateful for every time I showed up despite fear, fatigue, or doubt. Persistence is my silent promise to myself that I will see things through, no matter how long it takes. It is proof that my dreams matter and my purpose is worth the effort."

~Reflection~

51.

Gratitude for Joy in the Simple Things – Gratitude.

A.M. - "I give thanks for joy in the simple things, for they keep my heart light when troubles try to weigh me down."

Mid. - "Joy in the simple things is my daily anchor. Even when troubles come and try to cloud my mind, I find light in a smile, in a breeze, in the warmth of the sun — and I give thanks for it."

P.M. - "Every day, I give thanks for joy in the simple things — the smell of fresh air, the sound of laughter, the quiet of Daily light. There are days when troubles come, determined to limit my thinking and weaken my spirit. But joy in the simple things breaks their hold. It reminds me that life is still beautiful, that my heart can still be light, and that no shadow can fully erase the light I choose to see."

~Reflection~

52.

Gratitude for Inner Healing – Gratitude.

A.M. - "I give thanks for inner healing, knowing true change begins within before it can bloom outside."

Mid. - "I am grateful for the healing taking place within me. Many try to fix the outside first, but I know true healing starts inside — in the heart, in the mind, in the spirit — and grows outward."

P.M. - "This morning, I give thanks for inner healing — the quiet work that happens in the heart, mind, and spirit long before it shows on the outside. So often, people try to heal their surroundings, their image, or their circumstances without tending to the wounds within. But I know that lasting transformation begins inside. I honor the process, the patience, and the grace it takes to heal myself from the inside out. My gratitude is for every layer of me that chooses wholeness over hurt."

~Reflection~

53.

Gratitude for Patience – Gratitude.

A.M. - "I give thanks for patience, for it holds the grace I need to see my desires fulfilled in their perfect time."

Mid. - "Today, I am grateful for patience — the quiet strength that keeps me steady. Without it, frustration can take over. With it, I carry the grace to keep going until my desires manifest."

P.M. - "This morning, I give thanks for patience — the gentle yet powerful gift that holds me steady when life feels slow or uncertain. I know that sometimes frustration comes when I lose patience, when I forget that everything worth having blooms in its own time. Patience is not passivity; it is grace in motion. It keeps me aligned with my vision without forcing what is not yet ready. Today and every day, I honor patience as the bridge between my faith and my fulfillment."

~Reflection~

54.

Gratitude for Boundaries – Gratitude.

A.M. - "I give thanks for strong, intentional boundaries — the foundation that keeps my life steady and safe."

Mid. - "I am grateful for boundaries that protect my peace and uphold my worth. Without a firm foundation, nothing can stand. My boundaries make sure my life remains steady."

P.M. - "This morning, I give thanks for boundaries — the intentional, strong, and unwavering lines that hold my life together. Just like a structure cannot stand without a solid foundation, my peace and purpose cannot last without boundaries. They are not walls of fear, but pillars of protection, respect, and self-love. With my boundaries in place, I build a life that can weather storms and remain standing."

~Reflection~

Gratitude for Self-Worth – Gratitude.

A.M. - "I give thanks for my self-worth, for it allows me to see my true value and live at my fullest potential."

Mid. - "Self-worth is the foundation for how I see and treat myself. I give thanks for the balance and strength it brings, knowing it shapes my thoughts, my choices, and my future."

P.M. - "This morning, I give thanks for self-worth — the inner knowing that I am valuable, capable, and deserving of good things. Without it, I might minimize myself when I should stand in my fullness. With it, I think differently about my potential, my opportunities, and my place in the world. Balanced self-worth keeps me from settling for less than I deserve and empowers me to move toward all that I am meant to be. Today, I honor my worth, and I let it guide me into everything I am capable of accomplishing."

~Reflection~

56.

Gratitude for Self-Love – Gratitude.

A.M. - "I give thanks for self-love, the key to becoming, to resilience, and to living free from the mercy of others' approval."

Mid. - "Self-love is the foundation of my becoming. I give thanks for the way it frees me from begging for love in harmful places, and for the discernment it gives me to protect my empathy from misuse."

P.M. - "This morning, I give thanks for self-love — the key to my becoming, the root of my resilience, and the shield that protects my empathy. I know many remain stuck because they return to familiar places, even when those places are not good for them, hoping someone else will give them the love they should give themselves. Without self-love, kindness is exploited, boundaries are crossed, and discernment is dulled. With self-love, I see my value clearly. I know when to give and when to withdraw. I am no longer at the mercy of others' love, because I am already full within. Today, I honor that love, and I let it shape every choice I make."

~Reflection~

Gratitude for Self-Trust – Gratitude.

A.M. - "I give thanks for self-trust, for it allows me to move with confidence, knowing I can rely on my own wisdom."

Mid. - "Self-trust is my anchor. I give thanks for the courage it gives me to choose, to act, and to stand by my decisions without fear or regret."

P.M. - "This morning, I give thanks for self-trust — the deep, unshakable knowing that I can depend on my own wisdom, instincts, and choices. Without it, doubt creeps in, voices from the outside grow louder, and I become uncertain of my own path. With it, I stand firm. I make decisions with clarity, I move forward with confidence, and I know that even if I stumble, I will find my way. Self-trust frees me from living at the mercy of others' opinions and anchors me in my own truth."

~Reflection~

58.

Gratitude for Self-Discipline – Gratitude.

A.M. - "I give thanks for self-discipline, the power that turns my abilities into results and keeps me moving, even alone."

Mid. - "I am grateful for self-discipline — the strength that gets things done, protects my peace, and shocks those who thought I'd stay stuck. It keeps me steady even without applause."

P.M. - "This morning, I give thanks for self-discipline — the force that transforms my abilities into real results. So often, what we fail to achieve is not due to lack of skill, but lack of discipline. Without it, people drift into situations they regret, sometimes ones they can never undo. With discipline, I become different, unpredictable, impossible to hold down. It allows me to keep my life in purer, more sacred spaces — free from interruption, regret, or self-doubt — even when no one is rooting for me. Discipline is my silent strength, my personal victory, and my constant ally."

~Reflection~

59.

Gratitude for Self-Accountability – Gratitude.

A.M. - "I give thanks for self-accountability — the courage to own my choices so my future self can be proud, not disappointed."

Mid. - "Self-accountability is not impossible, but it requires courage. I give thanks for the strength to follow through, to own my actions, and to advocate for myself now so my future self will thank me."

P.M. - "This morning, I give thanks for self-accountability — the challenging but powerful choice to own my actions, my decisions, and my results. Too often, people avoid it, preferring to blame others rather than take responsibility for what belongs to them. But accountability is a gift to myself. It is me advocating for my own success, setting a standard for who I am, and ensuring my future self is grateful for my actions, not burdened by my neglect. I honor accountability as the pathway to integrity, growth, and self-respect."

~Reflection~

60.

Gratitude for Adaptability – Gratitude.

A.M. - "I give thanks for adaptability — the skill to adjust when needed and the wisdom to know when not to."

Mid. - "Adaptability is survival. I give thanks for the ability to adjust to what serves me while recognizing that not everything deserves my adaptation."

P.M. - "This morning, I give thanks for adaptability — the ability to survive, grow, and thrive by adjusting to new conditions. Many resist change because it demands adaptation, but I see it as a strength. To adapt is to find my best way forward, yet I also honor the wisdom to know that not everything requires my adjustment. Some environments are meant to be left as they are, while I remain true to myself. Adaptability is my balance between flexibility and integrity."

~Reflection~

61.

Gratitude for Courage – Gratitude.

A.M. - "I give thanks for courage — the audacity to face what others avoid and to move forward despite fear."

Mid. - "Courage is not for everyone. I give thanks for the audacity to be brave, to take risks, and to stand firm even when it's easier to retreat."

P.M. - "This morning, I give thanks for courage — the fire that pushes me forward when comfort tempts me to stay still. Not everyone has the audacity to be courageous, to step into the unknown, to face challenges without guarantees. But courage is my companion. It reminds me that fear can exist without controlling me, that risks can be worth the reward, and that standing firm in my truth is always worth it. I honor my courage as a gift and a responsibility."

~Reflection~

62.

Gratitude for Progress – Gratitude.

A.M. - "I give thanks for every step forward — small or big — for progress is proof I'm moving toward my destiny."

Mid. - "Every bit of progress matters. I give thanks for how far I've come, knowing it's greater than how far I have left to go. I will get there, no matter what."

P.M. - "This morning, I give thanks for progress — every step forward, whether small or big. Progress keeps me from the brink of destruction, from standing still in places that no longer serve me. I choose to celebrate how far I've come instead of being frustrated about how far I still have to go. The truth is, where I am now is already a victory over where I once was. My progress is a promise that I will reach my destination, no matter the pace, no matter the obstacles."

~Reflection~

Gratitude for Endurance – Gratitude.

A.M. - "I give thanks for endurance — the strength to not just start, but to keep going until I finish strong."

Mid. - "Endurance is my power to see things through. I give thanks for the strength to keep moving toward my dreams, my goals, and my divine walk — all the way to completion."

P.M. - "This morning, I give thanks for endurance — the unshakable strength that allows me to not only begin but to keep going until I finish what I started. Endurance is what carries me through challenges, delays, and doubts, ensuring I reach my goals, complete my projects, and honor my divine walk. Many can start, but not all have the heart to keep going. I am grateful that I do. Endurance keeps me faithful to my vision and committed to the finish line."

~Reflection~

64.

Gratitude for Focus – Gratitude.

A.M. - "I give thanks for focus — the clarity that frees me from traps and keeps me moving toward my vision."

Mid. - "Focus protects me from psychological traps that keep me stuck. I give thanks for the discipline to sometimes live like an island so my vision stays clear and my goals stay in reach."

P.M. - "This morning, I give thanks for focus — the ability to direct my energy toward what truly matters without being pulled into distractions or psychological traps. Sometimes, to stay focused, I must live like an island — distant from noise, detached from drama. It may feel hard at first, but I know it is possible and necessary. Focus is my commitment to my vision, my shield against what wastes my time, and my assurance that I am moving toward the life I am meant to live."

~Reflection~

65.

Gratitude for Consistent Vision – Gratitude.

A.M. - "I give thanks for consistent vision — the clarity that keeps me moving toward my purpose without quitting too soon."

Mid. - "Many want abundance and success, but their vision is blurred by noise and distractions. I give thanks for a consistent vision that keeps me focused, patient, and ready to seize real opportunities."

P.M. - "This morning, I give thanks for consistent vision — the steady, unshakable clarity that guides my steps toward abundance, health, wealth, and fulfilling experiences. I know that without it, the noise of unnecessary chatter and distractions can blur my path. Too many quit too soon, missing the opportunities that were just within reach. My consistent vision keeps me moving forward, keeps me patient, and ensures I arrive at what is meant for me without being swayed or discouraged."

~Reflection~

66.

Gratitude for Divine Alignment – Gratitude.

A.M. - "I give thanks for divine alignment — where vision, focus, and purpose work together for my highest good."

Mid. - "Divine alignment is never too late, too much, or not enough. I give thanks for the way it unites my vision, focus, and purpose, removing glitches and distractions so I can rise higher."

P.M. - "This morning, I give thanks for divine alignment — the sacred state where vision, focus, and purpose flow together for my highest good and greatest elevation. It is never too late, too much, or not enough; it is always exactly what I need. Divine alignment removes glitches, silences nonsense, and clears the path so I can go beyond limitations. In this alignment, I am unstoppable, grounded in truth, and fully supported as I rise."

~Reflection~

67.

Gratitude for Clarity of Purpose – Gratitude.

A.M. - "I give thanks for clarity of purpose — the gift that keeps my loyalty true and my steps intentional."

Mid. - "Clarity of purpose is a grace I do not take lightly. It guides my loyalty, helps me control the chaos, and reminds me to take life one day and one step at a time."

P.M. - "This morning, I give thanks for clarity of purpose — a gift and a grace that shapes every choice I make. It tells me where my loyalty belongs and keeps me from scattering my energy in the wrong places. With this clarity, I control the chaos instead of being consumed by it. I take life one day at a time, one step at a time, using my time wisely, effectively, and intentionally. No more clout chasing, no more wasting what is precious. My purpose is clear, and my path is sure."

~Reflection~

68.

Gratitude for Time Well Invested – Gratitude.

A.M. - "I give thanks for time well invested, knowing every moment spent with purpose will return something good."

Mid. - "There is no greater loss than wasted time. I give thanks for time well invested — with loved ones, my community, or myself — knowing it always yields something meaningful."

P.M. - "This morning, I give thanks for time well invested. I know that time wasted is gone forever, but time invested returns blessings, lessons, and joy. Whether it's with friends, family, siblings, community, or in solitude with myself, I value the moments that carry intention. When my time is invested with purpose, I know something good will always come from the experience. I honor my time as the rare treasure it is."

~Reflection~

Gratitude for Valuable Connections – Gratitude.

A.M. - "I give thanks for valuable connections — the kind that strengthen me, align with me, and have my back."

Mid. - "Not all connections are good ones. I give thanks for valuable connections that share my values, strengthen my spirit, and make me more fearless in pursuing my path."

P.M. - "This morning, I give thanks for valuable connections — the relationships that align with my vision, my values, and my purpose. I've learned that some characters may seem alike at first, only to reveal themselves as far from my ideologies. But valuable connections are different; they strengthen me, inspire me, and give me the confidence of knowing someone has my back. I will not allow history to repeat itself. I make adjustments where needed, protect my circle, and cherish the connections that truly matter."

~Reflection~

70.

Gratitude for This Moment – Gratitude.

A.M. - "I give thanks for this very moment — for the time I've taken to speak life into myself today."

Mid. - "Even this moment is a gift. I give thanks for the time I've spent declaring life over myself, for choosing to feed my spirit, and for making space to honor who I am becoming."

P.M. - "This morning, I give thanks for this very moment — for the time I've taken to speak life, truth, and gratitude into myself. Every word is an investment in my spirit, a reminder that I am worthy of the love, focus, and intention I give to others. I am grateful for the space I've created here, for the breath between thoughts, for the chance to affirm my worth and my path. In this simple act, I have honored myself, and that alone is something to be deeply thankful for."

~Reflection~

71.

Gratitude for Accountability

A.M. - "I am grateful for accountability — it keeps me aligned with my goals and reminds me of what must be done."

Mid. - "Without accountability, progress is a guess. I give thanks for the clarity that comes from knowing where I am, what stage I'm in, and what I'm willing to do to get where I need to be."

P.M. - "I am deeply grateful for accountability, for it is the bridge between intention and accomplishment. Without it, dreams remain ideas and progress remains out of reach. I choose to know where I stand, to be honest about my stage, and to be clear about what I'm willing to do in order to arrive at the place my spirit is called to. Accountability is my anchor — it ensures I do the work, finish the work, and live the results of the work. Today, I walk in the discipline of accountability and honor the path I have chosen."

~Reflection~

72.

Gratitude for Awareness

A.M - "I give thanks for awareness — the ability to see clearly and choose wisely."

Mid. - "Awareness keeps me from repeating cycles. I am grateful for the clarity to recognize what serves me and what does not."

P.M. - "This morning, I give thanks for awareness — the gift that allows me to observe, discern, and choose with intention. Awareness keeps me from living on autopilot and empowers me to respond instead of react. With awareness, I move consciously and protect my future."

~Reflection~

73.

Gratitude for Willingness

A.M - "I give thanks for willingness — the openness to grow, change, and evolve."

Mid. - "Nothing shifts without willingness. I am grateful for the courage to be open to learning and doing better."

P.M. - I rise in gratitude for willingness — the inner yes that allows transformation to begin. I am willing to learn, to release what no longer serves me, and to grow beyond who I was yesterday. This willingness keeps me aligned with progress."

~Reflection~

74.

Gratitude for Inner Strength

A.M - "I give thanks for my inner strength — steady, quiet, and reliable."

Mid. - "Even when life challenges me, my inner strength holds. I am grateful for the power that lives within me."

P.M. - "This morning, I honor my inner strength — the resilience that has carried me through moments no one else saw. It is not loud, but it is unbreakable. I am grateful for the strength that keeps me standing and moving forward."

~Reflection~

Gratitude for Direction

A.M - "I give thanks for direction — knowing where I'm headed even if the path unfolds slowly."

Mid. - "I am grateful for direction in my life. Even when the road isn't clear, I trust I am moving the right way."

P.M. - "Today, I give thanks for direction — the sense of guidance that keeps me from wandering aimlessly. I may not see every step, but I know I am being led. Direction gives me peace, confidence, and purpose."

~Reflection~

76.

Gratitude for Breath

A.M - "I give thanks for my breath — life moving through me right now."

Mid. - "Each breath is a reminder that I am alive, present, and capable. I am grateful for this moment."

P.M. - "This morning, I slow down and give thanks for my breath. With every inhale, I receive life. With every exhale, I release tension. Breath grounds me in now, where all power exists."

~Reflection~

Gratitude for Choice

A.M - "I give thanks for choice — the power to decide who I become."

Mid. - "No matter what happened before, I still have choice. I am grateful for the freedom to choose differently."

P.M. - "Today, I honor my power of choice. I give thanks that I am not trapped by my past, circumstances, or others' expectations. Each choice I make moves me closer to alignment and integrity."

~Reflection~

BONUS.

Gratitude for Becoming

A.M - "I give thanks for who I am becoming — steadily, intentionally, and truthfully."

Mid. - "I am grateful for my becoming. I am not rushing, and I am not stuck — I am unfolding."

P.M. - "This morning, I give thanks for the process of becoming. I honor the growth happening in me, even when it's quiet. I trust who I am turning into and allow myself to evolve without pressure or comparison."

~Reflection~

Conclusion

You've now spoken life into yourself for 77 days — or 77 moments — of AM Gratitude Galore. You've turned mornings into sacred ground, and you've reminded yourself that gratitude is not passive. It is active, intentional, and fiercely protective of your energy.

From here forward, never underestimate what a few seconds of powerful words can do for your day. Keep your gratitude as you keep your breath — constant, life-giving, and non-negotiable.

Let this not be the end of your practice, but the beginning of your next level. Continue to speak these words. Continue to rise. Continue to choose yourself. And so it is.

Scan here to explore a list of the author's books and collaborations.

Aha Moment

~Personal Reflection~

~Personal Reflection~

~Personal Reflection~

www.ingramcontent.com/pod-product-compliance
Lightning Source LLC
Chambersburg PA
CBHW081347040426
42450CB00015B/3342